Labradors

Labradors

Jane Eastoe

Illustrations by Meredith Jensen

BATSFORD

First published in the United Kingdom in 2022 by

B. T. Batsford Ltd
43 Great Ormond Street
London WC1N 3HZ

An imprint of B. T. Batsford Holdings Limited

ISBN: 9781849947930

A CIP catalogue record for this book
is available from the British Library.

10 9 8 7 6 5 4 3 2 1

Reproduction by Rival Colour Ltd, UK
Printed in Italy by L.E.G.O. SpA

Contents

Labradors

Introduction

Let me introduce myself: I am a labrador retriever, absolutely the best breed you could choose. I am very happy to meet you – do you mind if I give you a good sniff? Mmmm, you smell good. Have you got any food in your pockets? I'm really peckish. May I sniff you again? Sorry, I got distracted, my nose is one of my key senses. Do I smell food? FOOD! Is it time for dinner? I admit it, I have bit of an oral fixation, it's my thing.

Focus, I can focus. Actually, I am one of the cleverest and most obliging dog breeds you will meet. I can be trained to be a reliable working dog: acting as a guide dog and assistance dog; employed in search and rescue; retrieving for hunters or working in drug and explosives detection. I actively enjoy working and I am eager to please. In short, I am a sweet-tempered dog and only too happy to do anything my owner asks of me. My good nature makes me popular with families. I like children, and because I have a low prey drive (I'm not bred to chase things or to kill them), I can learn to live happily with other pets and to behave beautifully around other animals.

Labradors have been one of the most popular dog breeds in the United

Kingdom for the last 30 years; a survey conducted by Pet Plan in 2018 found that 12 per cent of all dogs in the United Kingdom were labradors. In 2022 I topped the American Kennel Club's poll as the most popular breed in the USA for the thirty-first time. I am beloved and my skills are utilized in many countries all around the world.

My breed was recognized by the British Kennel Club in 1903 and the American Kennel Club in 1917. Our origins are in Newfoundland, Canada, around the 16th century, where we worked tirelessly with fishermen, helping to retrieve nets and lost lines; we also pulled carts loaded with fresh fish. You might not have recognized us then because we were smaller than we are now. Our hardy ancestors were bred with hunting dogs belonging to the English nobility, producing the popular labrador breed of today around the 1830s. I am classified as belonging to the gundog group, along with spaniels, setters and pointers, to name a few.

I am what people politely call 'sturdy', and it must be said that if I am overfed, I can become obese. Have I mentioned that I love food? I have no sense of portion control and, left to my own devices, I will eat and eat and eat. I commonly weigh between 25 and 36kg (55–80lb). I have a broad skull, a kindly expression, a deep chest, strong legs, a keen sense of smell, and I can hold something in my mouth without hurting it. I can run for long distances with an easy loping stride. I benefit from plenty of exercise, and I can keep going all day if required, which is why I make a good working dog. Please don't underestimate my need for exercise.

My topcoat is thick and short, my undercoat is softer. I come in black, yellow and chocolate, though my tones can range from pale to dark within each shade – both Red Fox and white labs are genetically yellow. My thick coat means that I am tough and will happily go out in any weather. This also means that I have a lot of coat to moult. I shed hair with gay abandon! A daily brush will help ensure you don't find great clumps of my hair around your house, especially when I am moulting.

I am a high-energy dog, especially when I am young, though as a puppy it is important that you do not over-exercise me. As an adult dog I appreciate two one-hour walks, as a minimum, every single day, with lots of opportunity to play. I also really enjoy training. This is important because I am big and strong and when young I can wreak havoc if I'm not trained. I can, and will, drag you along in my wake if you don't train me to walk to heel.

I will chew anything and everything I can lay my teeth on (that oral fixation again). As a puppy, I will be incredibly boisterous, so start training me from day one. Initially, use food as a regular training aid, though I will learn to do what you want without food because I want to please you.

On the subject of eating, have I told you that I am an absolute gourmet? My idea of what is à la carte may, however, be somewhat different from yours. I will eat anything and everything I can lay my teeth into. A piece of rotten fish by the river – DELICIOUS! A chunk of wood – very tasty! A pile of dog poo or human poo – heavenly! Strangely enough, you don't seem very keen on this trait.

I LOVE your socks, they smell deliciously of you, and I will consume them with great relish, especially as a puppy. This is very bad for me and can result in an expensive trip to the vet to excavate unsuitable items from my tummy or bowels. It is important that I learn what I am not allowed to eat from you. I will take instruction; however, every walk is an opportunity for me to unearth some other unspeakable titbit! Some of this wide-ranging diet will have an impact on my bowels – I have a tendency for flatulence.

While we are on the subject of scent, I am partial to a good roll in anything that smells particularly bad. Moreover, introduce a labrador into your household and you had also better get used to the smell of wet dog. There is nothing I enjoy more than swimming or wading in water. It is my idea of FUN! My thick coat stops me from feeling the cold and I use my tail like a rudder to steer. A pool of stagnant water, from which I will emerge smothered in pond weed and exuding the pong of rotten eggs, will suit me just fine. I am not picky about the quality of the water.

Please remember that you are in charge of me; I won't have much sense in the water because it is such fun, so you will need to limit my time and make sure that it is safe for me to swim, just as you would with a child. If you let me play in the water for too long, I can get what is known as 'limber tail'. Instead of wagging happily my tail will hang down because it is sore and painful for me to move.

Do I have a downside? I have to admit that because I am so devoted to you, I can develop separation anxiety. I can bark when you leave me and indulge in destructive behaviour because I am bored. However, if you give me sufficient exercise and are prepared to train me, I can learn to cope without you for stretches of time. Toys that keep me mentally engaged will help when I am young.

In addition, my breed has developed some unfortunate genetic characteristics, such as hip and elbow dysplasia, which makes it hugely important that you only purchase labrador retrievers from reputable dog breeders. By screening dogs carefully and only breeding from ones that do not appear to carry defective genes, it is hoped that in time these defects can be eliminated. The fact that a puppy is a registered pedigree breed does not confirm that its parents have been screened for abnormalities. A good labrador breeder will be happy to discuss the issues with you and to show a paperwork trail.

It perhaps speaks volumes that despite these issues I remain a hugely popular dog. Why? Because I will love you unconditionally. I will be the best friend you have ever had. I don't criticize or hold grudges: in my eyes you are practically perfect in every way, which makes me even more lovable. When you sit down, I will sit beside you, lay my head on your lap and gaze deep into your eyes. I worship and adore you with every fibre of my being. You are the centre of my world, and what could be nicer than that?

Holly

Owned by Shelby | Lives in Melbourne, Australia | @_house.of.holly

Holly is a busy girl, working as a medical
assistance dog while also enjoying various sports,
including dock diving. Her favourite things to do
are swim and play fetch.

Puppies

I don't like to brag, but when it comes to puppies there really is nothing, absolutely nothing, cuter than a labrador puppy! We feature in advertisements for good reason; we are irresistible. We tear around like mad things, tripping over our own feet, tails wagging enthusiastically. We are delighted and excited by everything we see and we love to explore. Our fur is soft and too big for our small bodies, our eyes big and melting, and our soft mouths look exactly like the embroidered muzzle of a beloved cuddly toy. In fact, that's exactly what we look like!

Only buy a labrador puppy from a reputable breeder. As mentioned earlier, our breed, like many others, can be affected by some inherent genetic weaknesses, such as progressive retinal atrophy, which leads to premature blindness, and hip or elbow dysplasia, which cause lameness and severe pain. Sadly, these are not rare disorders, but there are other issues that breeders can screen for too, including centronuclear myopathy (CNM), a muscle wasting disease, and exercise-induced collapse (EIC). Reputable breeders will have their dogs screened in an effort to eliminate these genetic disorders from

their litters. Puppies purchased online from puppy farms will not have received this level of care and attention.

When you come to meet us for the first time you will be questioned carefully by the breeder about what you want from us. Do you want a show dog, a working dog or a pet? What kind of a pet do you want: loving or lively? Depending on your answers you may only be shown a couple of puppies to choose from that best suit your requirements.

You should meet my mother and quite possibly some of my other relatives too. My father might not be around to view as he may live some distance away, but you should see a picture of him at least.

A litter of labrador puppies is adorable but let me give you some words of wisdom: even if you plan to have two dogs, don't get them from the same litter at the same time, no matter how great the temptation. Labrador puppies are a handful; we are playful, clumsy, strong, boisterous, we chew anything and everything and need masses of exercise and attention. If you take me and one of my siblings, we will become very reliant on one another and pay you little heed. What's more, as we mature, we may fight to determine which is the dominant labrador in the pack. If you want two labradors (and why wouldn't you?), start with one and get a second only when the first is well-trained. The first dog will lead the way with all the basic training techniques.

Preparing My Home

Once a sale has been agreed you should make a few preparations.

Arrange to take a good chunk of time off work to help your puppy settle in. The more secure I feel from the start the better your chance of reducing destructive behaviour. If you can't take much time off work, you will need to arrange for someone else to be with me. It is not fair to leave me alone for long when I am very small, though it is important you leave me for short spaces of time once I have got used to my new environment.

- **Security:** Please check that your garden has adequate fencing.

I am a great escapologist and when small I can, and will, wriggle through very small holes or gaps in the fencing. Repair as required or plug small holes with logs or chicken wire. Once I grow this will become less of an issue.

- **Bedding:** I will need a lovely soft bed, but at first you'll probably find that a big adult one may overwhelm me. Initially, it is good to have something with nice soft sides so that I am protected from draughts; this will also stop me slipping off in my sleep. Soft cloth baskets with tall sides and a cushion inside will suit me very well when I am little.

- **Crate:** You might want to get me a crate, not to keep me in, but to give me a nice safe bolthole. I will appreciate it if you cover this over with a blanket so it stays nice and warm, and a heated pad will simulate the warmth of my siblings. If you put paper, or a puppy pad on the floor of the crate I can relieve

myself in the night. I will never usually soil my bed, but accidents happen, and when I am very small I will need to pee during the night. Check my bedding in the morning to make sure it is dry, and please wash it if it is wet – we like to have clean bedding. You can shut the door at night, after I have been out for a pee. Then you can sleep easy in the knowledge that I can't run around in the night. In the daytime, a crate should not be used as a cage, although you can shut me in for short periods if you are going out.

- **Bowls:** Buy two food bowls, one for food and one for water, which you'll leave down for me the whole time. Stainless steel is durable and easy to keep clean.

- **Poo bags:** You should also purchase a supply of poo bags so you can dispose of my poo; compostable bags are available.

- **Toys:** Please buy me some toys. I will want to chew and I am very playful. If I start to nibble or nip your fingers, you can give me a toy to chew on instead – my teeth are like needles! I will get the message that one is acceptable and the other is not (see Chapter 2 for more detailed advice on training). Balls and soft toys are particular favourites – I love anything that squeaks but will remove all the stuffing with terrifying speed, and the squeaker must be taken away from me as it can be dangerous, so squeaky toys should only be allowed under supervision. I will still love the empty fluffy carcass

so don't throw it away! Harder toys are helpful for teething. As I already mentioned, I will put everything in my mouth, I will chew it, and I *will* destroy it.

- **Collar and lead** You may also want to get me a lightweight puppy collar and a lead, even though you won't actually be able to take me out for a walk for a few weeks. Until my vaccinations take effect, it is simply not safe for me to mix with other dogs, or to be anywhere that other dogs have been. However, please take me out and about with you. Carry me around – you will be mobbed like a film star because I am so cute. This is important socialization for me. Always make sure that you can slip two fingers underneath the collar when it is around my neck and remember to check regularly: I will grow quickly and tight collars are uncomfortable. If you put a collar around my neck early on, and put me on the lead to play, I will get used to it before you take me out on my first walk.

House Rules

It is a good idea to agree house rules in advance of my arrival. Am I going to have the run of the house, be limited to the downstairs or only be allowed in certain rooms under supervision? Am I going to be allowed on the sofa or the beds? As a dog with an oral fixation and a genetic tendency to obesity, a good rule would be never to give me treats from the table. I need consistency and clarity and will constantly challenge boundaries.

Please scour the house in advance for things that I might chew or eat that could be harmful. I am like a toddler and cannot be trusted to be sensible, quite possibly for the next two to three years!

Training Basics

Training starts from day one, but before you leap to Chapter 2, make sure that everyone in your household grasps the basic principles. Agree together in advance what specific training words you will use; I will grasp clear, one-word instructions much faster. Use 'Sit' – not 'Sit down'; if you want me to lie down on the floor say 'Down' – not 'Lie down'; 'Wait' if you want me to stay in one

Things to Hide Out of Sight:

- Your shoes
- Electric wires, plugs and cables, your mobile phone, TV remote controls
- Your socks
- Children's toys
- Your shoes
- Medicine or chocolate in your handbag or briefcase, or lying around
- Your socks
- Slug pellets, mouse traps and garden chemicals
- Your shoes
- Painkillers
- Your socks
- Cleaning products – plastic bottles are very tempting to chew
- Your underwear – potentially highly embarrassing should I appear in front of your guests with a pair of pants in my mouth, plus I may eat them.

place until summoned; 'Stay' – if you want me to remain where I am until *you* return to me; and 'Leave' if you want me to let go of something. I will also need a trigger word for going to the toilet (see below).

House Training

Please familiarize yourself with the principles of house training a labrador in advance. Start collecting newspapers or buy puppy pads in preparation. It is much harder to house train any dog when the weather is cold than when it is warm and you can leave doors open all the time.

Don't leave me in the garden by myself. I like to be with you so will only worry about where you've gone and not focus on weeing or pooing. Please stay outside with me. That way you can give me lots of praise when I do the deed.

While I am a puppy, I will probably want to pee every time I wake up from a sleep and also to pee and or poo straight after every meal, so take me outside as much as you can. Every time I use the outdoor facilities, I am making scents that will trigger a similar response next time. As a general rule, I need to be taken outside every two hours – hourly is even better. Try to stay outside with me for a bit after I have done my business, play with me and let us have some fun – you are rewarding me for being good.

Agree on a key word you will use for toilet training – make this a word you don't use frequently in general conversation – my owner uses 'Bumbles'! Use the agreed word when I am peeing or pooing, say it over and over again quietly and gently. Don't tell me that I am a 'Good girl' or a 'Good boy' as this may become my trigger phrase to urinate.

I will quickly learn that when you use this trigger word you want me to wee or poo – such as last thing at night or before you are about to leave me in the house when you are going out. If everyone does this, I will learn what you want me to do much faster. Make a HUGE fuss of me every time I pee or poo out of doors, I need to understand that you are happy when I do this!

Make a mental note of where I like to pee outside and take me to that area when you want me to use the facilities. Some dogs like a dry surface, such as gravel, stone or concrete, some will only wee on short grass – we all have our preferences.

At night I can last for about 4–5 hours without weeing. Some owners set an alarm to take their puppy out; others keep one ear open and whisk us outside if they hear us wriggling. It all depends on where I am sleeping.

If I do have an accident don't shout at me. Say 'NO!' loudly if you catch me in the act and carry me into the garden, then praise me effusively when I wee. Labradors are sensitive to their owner's moods and hate to upset them. Shouting will only frighten me and make me nervous. It might also make me hide away when I need to wee, which will just compound the problem as you might not notice.

Gentle handling is required and lots of praise and rewards when I get things right. Labradors are smart, so I will catch on quickly. Clean up the accident area with an enzymatic cleaning material; biological washing powder mixed with warm water in a ratio of 1:9

will remove the smell. If you don't do this, I will be tempted to return to the same spot. Household disinfectants should be avoided as they contain ammonia and the smell of this may encourage me to soil the same area again.

The Journey Home

Puppies usually leave their families from the age of eight weeks old, by which time I will be weaned, but be prepared, as I may come with a list of dietary requirements for the first few months, and my breeder should give you some of the kibble I have been eating to help me settle in with you. This should help avoid tummy upsets. I will also have been microchipped, wormed and may have had my first inoculation. You will also be given my Kennel Club documents which have full details of my lineage.

The journey to my new home may be trying. Remember, I have probably never been in a car before, and I may cry for my siblings. I may be car sick; I might pee or even poo. On the other hand, I might just fall asleep on your lap

and stay that way for the whole journey. It is a good idea to have some old towels and kitchen roll to hand so you can easily deal with all eventualities. You might even want to pack a change of clothes – don't wear anything precious!

If I am car sick, I will grow out of it. Long term, we labradors tend to be good travellers; we enjoy a car journey and survey the landscape with interest. We long to stick our heads out of the window, tongue lolling, so that our senses are overwhelmed by all the wonderful smells on the air. Be careful where you allow me to do this – it's best restricted to when you are travelling at lower speeds and on country roads.

If I am car sick as a puppy, don't let me develop a phobia about the car. Keep putting me in it for a few minutes. Stay with me; give me treats. We don't need to go anywhere. Then take me round the block a few times on a short journey so I learn that being in the car is not a scary experience.

When we arrive home for the first time, put me down in the garden to give me a chance to relieve pent up tensions! Stay with me!

Welcome to Your New Home

When you bring me into the house, put me down and let me sniff around for a little while. Please don't overwhelm me with attention, especially if there are children in the house. Let me go to them and sniff them; let me take things at my own pace. This will be a frightening experience. Show me my bed and some toys. Show me where my water bowl can be found. When I have had a little time, give me something to eat, then take me outside straight away and give me the chance to do my business.

The First Night (Start As You Mean To Go On)

Given the choice I will sleep with you, in your bed. I will be sad and lonely without my siblings and without you. I will cry, I may wail and I may even emit an eerie howl. If you can't cope with this, keep me close for a few nights until I have settled in. Some people tuck the puppy bed beside theirs, so that they can offer a comforting stroke. I will get used to sleeping by myself in time.

Give me a nice small cosy bed initially; I will appreciate one with sides so I can rest my back against it as I did with my siblings. It also eliminates draughts. I will grow out of it, but it will help me settle in, and if you can put it in the washing machine so much the better!

Healthy Eating

After the first night with me, it will be time to tackle my dietary requirements. Labrador puppies have four small meals a day once they are weaned. My breeder should give you a sample menu and some of the packet food I have been eating to avoid any tummy upsets due to dietary changes. Don't change things around until I am settled and happy in my new home.

Labradors are naturally greedy dogs, so I will usually gobble up every last morsel. If I don't eat, keep an eye on me – I may be unwell. Lift my food bowl up after ten minutes and don't offer me food until my next mealtime. If I am still not eating after 24 hours, you may need to get me checked out by the vet.

As a small puppy, I will need four meals a day, nicely spaced out. At 12

weeks I can drop to three meals a day, and at six months I will be ready for just two meals a day. I will be fully grown from around 15–18 months, when I can go onto adult food as I will not require the same nutrients that I did when I was actively growing.

Recall

Start working on this as soon as you have settled on my name. Have treats to hand. Call my name in a slightly higher-pitched voice than usual and sound excited. When I come to you reward me with a treat and make a *HUGE* fuss of me. Let me go then repeat. If I don't come to you, try running away from me and call me – reward me when I come. Make it a fun game. Stick to my name only – no other words, not 'Here', not 'Come', just my name.

Treats

Keep treats strictly for training purposes. Don't give me anything off your plate, as much as I gaze at you with big, hopeful eyes. This will be hard because as I grow, I will become an expert in emotional blackmail. Try to remain resolute. Once you have fed me from your plate, I will thereafter expect a taste of everything.

The Vet

Most vets like you to register with them as soon as you get a puppy. They will give me a once-over to check I am doing okay, weigh me, test my microchip, get my vaccination schedules in place and discuss flea and tick treatments. They will also make a fuss of me so that my trip to the vet is a positive experience. Vets will probably know about puppy-socialization classes in the area, and usually have lists of useful contacts for the future, such as kennels and dog sitters.

The vaccination schedule varies slightly from country to country, so be guided by your vet. Some diseases require me to have an annual booster to ensure continued protection. The vet will advise you and will normally send out a reminder. All these diseases are extremely unpleasant and are easily passed on. Please make sure I am vaccinated as a puppy and that you maintain my annual booster-jab schedule to keep me safe.

Keep my vaccination certificates. The vet can update them as required and you will have to show them if you need to put me into kennels. No reputable kennels can take an unvaccinated dog.

A rabies vaccination is required in some countries and will be needed if you intend to travel internationally with me. This is not a quick process; rabies vaccinations need time to become effective and I have to have blood tests to ensure I have sufficient immunity. Allow an absolute minimum of 6–8 months for this process. You will also need to ensure that I have annual rabies boosters.

Vaccinations

The following vaccinations are required in most countries:
- Canine distemper
- Hepatitis
- Leptospirosis
- Parvovirus

JoJo

Owned by Ken | Lives in Plandome, New York | @jojotheblacklab

Smart, loyal and one of the happiest dogs you
will ever meet, JoJo is a wonderful companion,
guaranteed to put a smile on our faces. She is
just as happy retrieving as she is laying at
our feet.

Collar and Lead

While I am in quarantine and have to be carried about in the big wide world, take the opportunity to get me used to both my collar and lead. Be forewarned, I will not enjoy this experience. Start with the collar, put it on for a few minutes, give me treats, then take it off. Once I have had a few days to get used to the collar, try me with the lead – a few minutes at a time for both, followed by lots of treats, please.

Walking

I love to race around the garden and the house. Let me do this as much as I like because I have the choice to stop and rest whenever it suits me. However, please don't take me out on long marches when I am little; it wears me out and it is not good for me, or my joints. Large dog breeds, such as labs, should not be over-exercised; jumping and agility is discouraged until we are more mature. As a general rule, five minutes exercise a day for each month of life, so a four-month-old puppy can have one walk of 20 minutes a day. Fitness and stamina are built up a little at a time. Puppies under three months don't need walks; their vaccinations won't usually have taken effect until this time anyway, so it shouldn't be an issue.

When I go for my first booster injections with the vet at a little over one year of age, ask for advice on

building up my exercise regime further, which by now should be up to one hour per day. When I get to be a senior dog and start slowing down, you may have to shorten my walks.

Social Niceties

All dogs benefit from puppy socialization as soon as their vaccination schedule permits. We labradors tend to be incredibly friendly. Submissive weeing is quite common when we are little – it's just our way of showing that we know our place – so outside socializing might be a good idea. Some of us can be quite nervous, so we require socialization classes even more. Be gentle: you might need to just sit and watch the class with us until

we look sufficiently interested in the proceedings.

When puppies mingle, expect a lot of butt sniffing. For some reason you humans seem to find this ritual impolite, but it is simply our way of saying hello, so try not to mind. Please don't tell us off for doing what comes naturally. It also teaches us to recognize the signals that another dog might not be so friendly – if a strange dog stands with a stiff body and tail, with its hackles rising and ears back, I have to learn to back off.

Puppy-socialization classes usually include some element of group training and help to teach you how to teach me to focus on you, even when there are lots of distractions around. The instructors will also teach you dog-training techniques. Let's be frank about this: these classes are as much for you as they are for me. You have to learn how to handle me effectively so I will behave beautifully for you. You might think I'll never learn how to do anything, but the dog trainer will show you, with terrifying ease, how easy it is to get me to do what you want.

Don't blame me if I behave badly – basically it's all down to you. Keep on with my training every day and just wait to see how smart I am. Remember, there are no bad dogs, just bad owners.

Always take poo bags out with you and treats – lots of them – it will help you to keep me focused on what you want me to do.

Nervous Puppies

Most labrador puppies are quite bold and bumptious, but others suffer from anxiety. It is very important that you expose me to a range of situations – busy roads, stations, cafés and parks – so that I can meet different men, women, children and dogs of all breeds, and get used to the strange noises around me. I need to see bicycles and wheelchairs, people in hats or carrying walking sticks; every experience will help me adjust to the wider world. Carry me if my vaccinations have not yet taken effect: don't wait to take me out and about with you.

If I am nervous of other dogs when I am old enough to go out and about, don't scoop me up out of harm's way. This will only reinforce the idea that I am in grave danger. Talk to other dog owners and ask if it is okay to stroke their pets and talk to them, but don't push me forwards. Let me see you being open and friendly and allow me to build my confidence at my own pace.

Separation Anxiety

All dogs are pack animals and are happiest when they have you, the pack leader, in their sights. We labradors are incredibly attached to our family and hate being left behind, so we can suffer from separation anxiety.

Try not to reinforce nervous behaviour from the start. If your puppy

hates being away from you, encourage it to play, then leave the room for a moment; carry on playing and popping in and out so she gets more confident that you will return.

The same applies to teaching me to get used to being home alone. Only leave me alone for a few minutes initially so I don't have the chance to panic. Tire me out before you leave so that, hopefully, I'll just fall asleep. Build up the time you leave me gradually, starting with just five minutes.

Give me a toy to play with, such as one filled with treats, so that I am kept busy and occupied and am not stressed because you aren't in sight. A Kong is very useful: you can fill the inside with meat and freeze it so that I have to work to release the lovely, tasty filling.

Many people allocate their labrador puppy a particular space in the house when they go out; stair gates will help to confine me and stop me wreaking havoc throughout the house.

This will be more of a problem when I am young; labradors can go through a particularly destructive phase around the age of one. Older labradors might be content with someone taking them out for a good walk around the middle of the day, but younger labs won't be able to cope with so much time alone. You may have to arrange for me to spend part of the day with a relative or friend or put me into doggy day care so that I have plenty of company, exercise and entertainment.

Dog charities recommend that no breeds are left alone for more than 4–5 hours at a stretch. If this is a problem, a labrador almost certainly isn't the right breed for you. If I am left on my own too much I will become bored, which can lead to me becoming very destructive. Actually, this is something of an understatement. If I am bored, I can destroy carpets, curtains and blinds, plaster, skirting boards, sofas and chairs and much, much more. Do not underestimate my capacity for destruction!

Digging

Most puppies like to dig, and labradors are no exception. Take heart from the fact that this is usually something we grow out of. If digging is a problem,

avoid giving me large bones that I may want to bury. Try to distract me with something more interesting when I start digging, or allow me to have one place where I can dig and take me to this spot if I start digging anywhere else.

Travelling Companions

If you take your labrador puppy on trains, buses and the Subway or Underground when he is small, he may be fearful at first, but he will get used to it and behave calmly. Car travel, though you might not think it, has more restrictions.

In the UK, the Highway Code states that dogs and other animals must be suitably restrained. The interpretation of this is quite loose, however, for your sake and mine, please ensure that proper restraints are in place. Quite apart from the fact that you adore me and don't want any harm to come to me, if we have an accident, please remember that if I come hurtling through the car at speed, I can injure or kill you in precisely the same way another human can if they are unrestrained in the rear of the car.

The most effective way to keep me safe is to have a crate in the back of your car to minimize the distance I can be flung in a crash. If you familiarize me with the crate at home, I will be perfectly content to travel in this. Dog harnesses that clip onto seat belts are available if a crate is not an option. These should not be used in the front seat as if an air bag goes off in an accident it could seriously harm your dog. Dog guards that stop me from clambering into the front of the car can be fitted, but ideally these should be used in conjunction with a crate.

Hormones and Bitches

As I move towards my first birthday and the end of puppyhood, the hormones start to kick in; in developmental terms, a one-year-old labrador is the equivalent of a 15-year-old human. Most female labradors will have their first season (pro-oestrus) between the ages of 9 and 12 months, but some can go into heat earlier than this. Vets advise that female labradors should have one season before they are spayed, so brace yourself that you are going to have to cope with at least one season.

Labrador bitches tend to come into heat every 6–8 months, however, the frequency of seasons can vary depending on when her first season begins. Very young bitches who come into heat should not be allowed to breed; it can be dangerous for them to have puppies before they are fully mature, around 18–24 months.

Your bitch will be on heat for around 21–28 days. She may well become cranky – and for good reason: her vulva will swell, as may her nipples, she will bleed, and she will also need to urinate more frequently. Labradors are acutely conscious of the fact that they are bleeding. Although they keep themselves very clean, nevertheless they will drop blood – not excessively, but there will be spots here and there. There are a number of ways of dealing with this, but please bear in mind that as well as being cranky, your labrador bitch will also be understandably clingy and want to be with you – isolating her in a room with hard flooring will make her miserable if she is used to being with you.

Nowadays, you can buy pants for bitches on heat. She can wear these in the house, but she may take great exception to this addition to her wardrobe – remember, it will stop her from keeping herself clean. You can cover her bedding and the sofa with towels and wash them regularly, and you can cover carpeted areas of the floor with towels or newspaper. You can spot clean spots as they appear and then have your carpet professionally cleaned when she has finished her season. Try not to let any irritation show, as she will pick up on this.

Keep her in close contact when she is on heat: male dogs will find her irresistible and they can pick up her pheromone-filled scent from a long way away. Only let her off lead when you can do so safely or choose to walk her at times of the day when there will be fewer dogs around to bother her.

If you also have a complete male dog in the house, your life is about to get very difficult. One option is to persuade a friend to look after your male dog until your bitch has finished her season, or alternatively, you can keep your dogs

apart. The use of stair gates or crates can allow the two dogs to still see each other, but not to interact.

Neutering your labrador bitch once she has had her first season will give her protection against some forms of cancer and infection of the uterus (pyometra). She does not need a litter of puppies to be happy.

Some bitches can get very uncomfortable when they are on heat and a trip to the vet may be required. The vulva can become painfully swollen and her constant cleaning can aggravate this problem. If her nipples become distended, she may be producing milk and will require medication to stop production.

Once your labrador bitch has had her first season, speak to the vet about having her neutered. This is a straightforward operation and dogs recover very quickly. There is a cost involved, but a litter of unwanted puppies is far, far more expensive. Leave breeding pedigree puppies to the professionals. If you plan to breed from your bitch, make sure you seek professional advice from a breeder:

there is a lot to learn and health issues to be screened for, in addition to the complex business of birthing.

Hormones and Male Dogs

Most male labradors are fertile before they are fully grown, somewhere between 15 and 18 months of age. However, some are capable of siring puppies much earlier – you have been warned! Responsible breeders don't like male dogs to breed before the age of two, as they need to see how big he will be when fully grown; this can affect which bitch he is paired with.

Just like teenage boys, we sometimes act before we think – the testosterone is surging! In fact, for a short while, young male dogs have more testosterone than adult dogs, and this can lead to a sudden outbreak of territorial behaviour. Scent marking territory is an early indication of sexual maturity: if your male labrador continually stops for short wees to signal where he has been, this is scent marking. You may also find to your horror that a perfectly house-trained labrador suddenly lets you down by peeing inside a friend's house, or in a shop or a pub. This can happen with all breeds, not just labradors. Please always own up to my offence and offer to clean up my puddle.

Perfectly amiable labradors can suddenly start having stand-offs with other dogs. Don't panic, this doesn't necessarily mean your sweet boy is going to become an aggressive monster. Male dogs have to deal with a whole new set of signals from other males, who may suddenly be aggressive with them. Your puppy needs to learn to reevaluate the social signals he is getting. He will learn. Labradors tend not to be aggressive dogs.

If you are having to deal with some aggression for the first time, try not to panic. You will need to exercise your dog well and increase training; reinforcing good behaviour will help. If you are struggling, seek help from a professional dog trainer, they will have strategies that will help you and your labrador to cope.

A large number of dogs that are given up for rescue are adolescents and a labrador will not be mentally mature until three years of age. Just as for humans, this can be a challenging time for behaviour, so help your puppy move smoothly through to adulthood with kindness, plenty of exercise and lots of positive training. He or she will reward you in the long term.

Training

Labradors may be, quite simply, the very best working-dog breed in the world. We guide blind people, work as hearing dogs and therapy dogs, sniff out explosives and endlessly retrieve for our hapless owners who seem quite unable to find anything, see anything, hear anything or smell anything without our assistance – I mean honestly, it's right there in front of you! However, don't assume that I will develop such splendid characteristics without your assistance. Service dogs receive hours and hours of training. They learn to be helpful, polite and biddable and, being intelligent and fully

mentally occupied, they thoroughly enjoy their work. They understand what is expected of them and want nothing more than to please their owners.

To achieve this state of canine nirvana, you must be top dog, the 'pack leader' whose rules I follow. If you don't assume this position by teaching me to do what you say, I will try to usurp you and assume the pack-leader position myself in an unspoken coup.

I am a terrible decision maker and, in an effort to keep you safe, I may loudly herald the arrival of each and every visitor to the house with a cacophony of barking. I may try to prevent their entry

by growling, or I may greet all-comers by throwing my considerable weight at them in a state of high excitement.

If I am not properly socialized, I may view all runners, cyclists and small children with grave suspicion and try to nip them at every given opportunity. I may decide that trains and buses, or certain noisy places are simply not safe for us and refuse to enter. It's not easy to shift a sizeable labrador who flatly refuses to budge.

Training me is the key to keeping me under control. The more you train, the better behaved I will become, but it is a long process. Guide dogs have almost two years of intensive training before they are ready to become an elite working dog. Moreover, not every labrador that is trained will make the grade; character comes into play and some dogs are simply not emotionally equipped for the work.

I tell you this because I want you to understand that labradors are not all well-behaved by nature; hard work on your part, and my temperament and character will influence my progress. However, the more you train me and keep me well exercised and mentally stimulated, the happier I will be. I enjoy having a job to do. You just have to teach me what my job is.

Dog Training

Attending puppy-socialization classes and dog-training classes will help us to develop a good relationship and will help you to teach me good manners and how to behave. Please remember that I do not speak your language; you will have to patiently teach me how to do what you want. I won't understand the words, but I will learn what you want me to do when you make certain sounds. Learning appropriate hand signals will help me to further understand what you want. Training dogs is not difficult, but it requires time and patience from you. Two short, five-minute sessions daily will help me learn; if you put in the effort, I will repay you (most of the time) by behaving beautifully.

Initially you can train me by using treats alone, but you can graduate to clicker training as you progress. Clickers are used as a training tool to mark good behaviour. This is a small device that

The Basic Rules of Dog Training

- It is your job to keep me under effective control. You must have a lead with you every time we go out on roads and when signage requests it – often when nesting birds are in the area or around livestock.
- Don't let me approach cyclists, runners or other dog owners unless invited. Always put me on the lead if you see a horse and rider.
- Don't let me race off lead on private land or through crops.
- Be safe around livestock. Check fields before entering so you are not caught unawares. Maintain a good distance from livestock and give them plenty of space. Cattle and horses can be quite curious about dogs and very protective if they have calves or foals. If livestock comes worryingly close, release me so that I can get away and you can too.
- Never let me worry or chase livestock.
- Always bag up my poo and carry it with you. This can be disposed of in special dog-poo bins or, if none are around, any public litter bin.
- Don't leave bags of poo on the path to pick up later or hang them from tree branches. It is too easy to forget them or lose them. Pick up as you go.
- Put an identification tag on my collar with your contact details on it. Put *your* name on it (not my name) and a phone number. Remember to update this and my microchip details if we move house.
- Keep my vaccination and worming treatments up to date.

Solo

Owned by Jordan | Lives in East Anglia | @foxredsolo

Kind-hearted and easy going, Solo is just as
happy curled up on the sofa as he is on a trek
on the Cornish coastal path. His loyal and
enthusiastic nature makes him a joy to be
around and there's not a day his silliness and
affectionateness hasn't made us smile!

you hold in the palm of your hand which emits a click when pressed, an audible pat if you like. When we hear the click, we know we have done something good and that we will get a treat. It is an effective reward system that flags up good behaviour and that we will be rewarded for it. The use of the clicker can be expanded to promote and encourage new and developing good behaviours every time you spot them. Don't point the hand holding the clicker at me; keep it by your side.

Start by putting a treat in your closed hand and hold the clicker in your other hand. I will nose and nibble your hand to try to get at the treat. When I stop doing this, click the clicker and at the same time open your hand so that I can access the treat. It's imperative that you get the timing of the clicks right: you only want to use it to reward good behaviour and it can take a bit of practice to master the technique efficiently. In time, you *may* be able to use the clicker alone as a reward, but this will take some effort on your part to achieve.

Recall

This is the first lesson and a basic piece of obedience: you call, I come running. Some of us learn to come to our names quickly and easily, others are rather more wilful.

Call my name and sound really excited. Just use my name, or the word 'Come', not 'Come here', or 'Here'. When I respond, reward me with a treat and make a HUGE fuss of me. I'll learn, really, really quickly.

Once I have grasped this, you may want me to come to you and sit, before I am rewarded (see technique below).

Even when you think we have mastered this technique, I guarantee I will let you down on occasion, and as teenagers (around 10–11 months old) we can become quite stroppy and uncooperative and develop selective hearing, just like humans.

If this happens, reinforce your original technique with lots of repetition. Call me back repeatedly and reward me with treats. You don't have to make me sit to get a treat. Instead, hold the treat in a clenched fist and make me touch your hand with my nose, then release the treat. Use the words 'Off you go' to tell me I can go away and play again. Repeat and repeat at random times throughout the walk.

If you only do this at the end of the walk, I will learn that it is not a good idea to return to you. It is best to get me on the lead before the end of the walk when I just think I am returning for another treat. Try to keep one step ahead of me mentally.

Lavish praise on me every time I come back to you, then give some more. As I become more reliable, you will notice that I keep looking back to check where you are. This is a good sign, as it indicates that I am attuned to you, that you are important to me and that I want to keep an eye on you so you don't suddenly disappear.

A whistle can be a very useful tool. It will save you from having to bellow my name. Plus, a whistle expresses no emotion, so I won't pick up on any anger in your voice if you are getting frustrated.

If am not behaving and run you ragged trying to catch me, don't ever shout at me when I finally come within grasp.

This will only make me apprehensive of returning to you – I won't understand why sometimes you give me a treat and sometimes you shout.

If I am proving to be very resistant to recall, try not feeding me before a walk and keep those treats to hand during the walk.

If I am still not responsive to recall, you can try hand-feeding my meals in the garden for about a fortnight. Your hands will get very messy, but I will follow you around devotedly as you feed me a little bit at a time. This helps to reinforce the message that you are the source of all good things and coming to you brings real benefits.

Long trainer leads are also an option. These are designed to drag along behind me as I run free but give you a better chance of catching me when you call. These are best used when you are able to stamp your foot on my lead. Call or whistle me in; if I don't respond immediately, pull me gently back in, reward me and release me.

If you call my name and I fail to return, don't keep calling me over and over again. Remember Fenton the labrador? He was famously filmed chasing deer in Richmond Park, London, while his owner could be heard futilely calling his name in desperation. The footage was put online and went viral. Fenton was in another zone and was not going to pay his master any attention, no matter how often his name was called.

If this happens, revert to basic training and perhaps consider some other form of training that encourages me to use my brain; agility or flyball classes might suit. Swimming for ten minutes is the equivalent to a one-hour walk, so take me to the beach if you can, or anywhere I can swim safely. Hide toys and make me work to find them or hide treats under beakers and make me work out where they are hidden.

As my name suggests, I love retrieving, so throw balls or frisbees, if you can throw a ball into a pond, so much the better. We labs are clever, if we are resistant to training techniques, some mental exercises might be just what we need.

Basic Commands

Keep training sessions short and please don't bother me with training if I have just had a meal, or if I am tired – all I will be interested in is sleeping and not learning. Pick the moment when I am likely to be at my most receptive. If I have just woken up and am doing high-speed circuits of the garden, you might also find it hard to keep me focused.

Sit

Put a treat in your hand in a fist. Hold your hand over my nose and say 'Sit'. Lift your hand slightly upwards and backwards – as I lift my nose up to follow the treat I will naturally drop my bottom and go into a sit. Praise me.

Once I have grasped this command, practice saying it with me beside you as well as in front of you.

Get me to sit before you give me my meals. As I become more disciplined you can make me wait to go to it until you give me the 'Off you go' command.

Down

Start this training once I have begun to grasp the 'Sit' command. For good results at the start, do this training where I can lie down comfortably, either on my bed or on a rug.

Get me to 'Sit' and reward me. Put another treat in the palm of your hand and say 'Down'. Then move your hand slowly towards the ground, edging it just out of reach as my nose follows your hand. I will lower my front legs and with a bit of luck my hindquarters will follow. If I get up to try to reach the treat, just pop me back in the 'Sit' position, give me a treat, then try 'Down' again. It might take a few attempts before I figure out what you want me to do.

Once I am beginning to grasp this instruction, you might like to introduce a hand signal to support it. With the treat in the palm of your hand, extend your index finger and point it downwards. Take the treat to my nose and repeat the same process with your hand so that I lie down. Make a huge fuss of me every time I get this right.

When I have grasped the basic principle, start practising the command away from my bed, I am quite well upholstered and will happily lie down on command virtually anywhere.

Wait

The 'Wait' command teaches me to stay where I am until you tell me what to do next. I'll stay in the car with this command while you find my lead and get me attached; without my knowing this command I might just leap past you and race off. I'll wait until you put my food bowl on the floor and won't almost knock you over in my effort to get at the food. I'll wait at gates and doors while you go ahead of me.

To teach me to 'Wait', first tell me to 'Sit', then take a step backwards, still facing me, holding your hand palm up, then call me to you. You'll probably have to do a lot of practice before I start waiting. Just keep up with short bursts of training and I'll get the message. Keep distances very small and gradually extend them as I am following the instruction reliably. It doesn't matter if I lie down instead of sitting, just so long as I stay put. In time you will be able to leave me sitting waiting while you walk a distance away and there I will remain until you call me.

Use 'Wait' every time you feed me. Make me sit, then tell me to wait until my food bowl is on the floor. I will keep getting up and try to rush it, but just raise the bowl in the air, put me back in the sit position and tell me to 'Wait' again. If you do this at each mealtime, it is an easy way of reinforcing the command.

Stay

'Stay' training starts in a similar way to 'Wait'. Put me in the sit position, take a step forwards with your right foot, holding your hand behind you with the palm facing me. I will probably get up and follow. Put me back in the sit position and try again. Eventually you will be able to take a step forwards, and then step back beside me without my moving.

Praise me effusively when I do as you have asked. Always try to walk off with your right foot leading for the 'Stay' command – this is a visual clue for me. It will be surprisingly difficult for you to maintain this small detail, but it is important – it sends me a clear signal that I am doing a 'Stay' exercise (you set off with your left foot instead when I am walking to heel).

As with teaching the 'Wait' command, extend the 'Stay' distance a little at a time. Keep repeating the word 'Stay' slowly, clearly and firmly. Turn and face me before you return to me. As I get even better at obeying you, when you have gone as far away from me as you wish, turn, face me and wait for five seconds before returning; continue to extend the time you wait at a distance: ten seconds, 20 seconds, 30 seconds, and so on.

In time you will be able to leave me, return to me and walk around my rear, with me remaining in a sit. I will be watching you closely the whole time. Always praise me calmly and quietly while I am still in position. Then release me with the 'Off you go' command.

Heel

Can I be blunt here? You move very slowly and when we are out on a walk there are things I want to see and smell. I will quickly grow into a big, powerful dog and will drag you along in my wake. This is a miserable experience for both of us; your arms will be pulled out of their sockets, and you won't feel like you are in control. I will be panting, gasping and choking as I nearly throttle myself in an attempt to go where I want, at the speed I want.

You need me to learn to walk comfortably beside you, with a slack lead, until you can let me off the lead and I can wander where I will. The sooner you can do this the better, so start my training in your garden before I am even allowed outside for a walk.

Decide which side you want me to heel to and stick to it. In competitive obedience training I should be on your left, and because I respond to visual clues you should always lead off with your left foot first to reinforce the message that we are walking to heel. Remember, you lead with your *right* foot when we are doing a 'Stay' exercise. From the start, these consistent visual clues help me to understand and differentiate between what you want me to do. If you don't intend to show me competitively, choose whichever side suits you best; left-handed people may naturally prefer to have their labrador heel to their right side (just remember to consistently lead off with the opposite foot when you are teaching me the 'Stay' exercise).

If you are heeling to your left, hold the loop of the lead in your right hand and use your left hand to keep my head level with your legs. Ultimately you are trying to keep my nose to the side of your leg. This may be too much of a challenge for me to begin with, but with lovely smelling treats in your hand, I should remain happily by your side.

Put treats in your left pocket, then reach up with your left hand, take a few treats and hold them in your fist. Let your hand hang by your side so that I can smell the treats and say 'Heel'. I will nose your hand in an effort to get at the treat. At very regular intervals give me a treat to keep me encouraged. Keep repeating the word 'Heel' over and over again while I am following your instruction.

Getting me to walk to heel will always be much easier on the way home as I will have had a good run around. You can also train me to 'Heel' in the garden off lead, but always have those treats to hand.

Gus

Owned by Meaghan | Lives in Vancouver, Canada | @gusinvancouver

Gus is an old soul who loves adventuring in the
mountains and is a total people pleaser. He's not
happy until everyone around him is smiling!

If I am being resistant to walking to heel, another technique you can employ is to keep changing direction without warning. This will throw me as I am expecting you to keep moving forwards. Every time I start pulling, change direction again. It doesn't make for the most productive walk in terms of distance, but it will reinforce the notion that I cannot always rely on you to plod along behind me. You are taking charge of our direction of travel. You are my pack leader.

If I am a very determined character, paying little heed to even the most patient heel training, you might want to consider purchasing some things to help. A double attachment body harness may discourage some labs from pulling, and if I am still resistant you could try a Halti training collar.

A Halti has linked sections that run around the back of my head as well as loosely around my muzzle. I can still drink and pant with a Halti collar on. Instead of the lead attaching to the collar on my neck, it is attached to a loop under my muzzle. You are guiding me by my nose and it is very hard for me to pull.

Please get me used to the Halti before you try to take me out with it on. Put it on me, give me treats, then take it off me. Keep doing this. I will probably try to pull it off with my paw or by rubbing along the ground. Don't let me keep doing this. Take it off, then put it on again a few minutes later, give me a treat, take it off and repeat.

If you hold the tip of your nose with your fingers and pull it sideways, you will see that your head automatically follows with no resistance. The Halti works on this principle. When I have worn a Halti consistently for a while you will discover that I automatically walk to heel without pulling.

If you have just the one labrador, you can work on my walking to heel quite efficiently, but if you have two, you may find that Haltis are the perfect solution to your problem.

Leave

This command is designed to make me give up something without a fuss. It can be a life-saver (quite literally) if I have made off with something dangerous, such as a bar of chocolate.

It can also have practical day-to-day advantages; we are natural retrievers and some labradors are very ball-focused. This can be a handy way of wearing us out quickly if you are short of time. However, it won't work as a strategy if you throw the ball once and I flatly refuse to give it up.

Start training me young by gently trying to remove a toy from my mouth. Say 'Leave' in a firm but kind voice. If I hang on to the toy don't pull – tug is a fun game in itself. Just produce another toy and make it seem more exciting than the one I am clutching in my jaw. Say 'Leave' again and offer me the new toy. If I drop the old toy, make a fuss of me and give me the new toy. Reinforce this message over and over again.

Overcoming Negative Behaviour

My character will determine how easy I am to train, but I am a labrador so together we should get there in the end. Never punish me for bad behaviour, no matter how angry you are, and reward me when I behave well. Labradors are very sensitive to mood, and we will be unhappy and frightened if you are angry.

Barking

If I go into energetic overdrive, and bark repeatedly whenever someone comes to the door, I may be being over-protective or desperate to welcome the visitor. Shouting, or trying to hold me back by the collar when you open the door won't help resolve the issue. Don't give me treats to distract me, because this will reward the barking; instead say 'Quiet' gently but firmly. When I stop barking, reward me.

Obviously, this doesn't help when you have someone at the door, so if I am causing mayhem, enlist a friend or neighbour to help. Get your friend to come to the door and make their presence known. When I start barking say 'Quiet' and wait until I stop, however long it takes. When I stop, give me a treat. Get your friend to knock or ring again, and repeat. This will take a little time, but I will catch on. If you can repeat this exercise for a couple of weeks, it will make a huge difference. The same method also works if I bark at other dogs when I am walking on the lead. Stop walking, say 'Quiet' and when I stop barking, reward me. Remember, I only get the reward when I am quiet.

If I bark when left alone, I may be suffering separation anxiety. This is not bad behaviour as such, though it may feel like it, especially if your lab is inclined to destroy the house in your absence. Don't be angry, your dog is genuinely frightened and unhappy.

If I am wide awake, bored and full of beans when you depart, I am more likely to be in a state of high anxiety. Always take me for a good walk before leaving me alone. If I am tired, I am more likely to be peaceful when you are out. After the walk, give me something I really like, such as a Kong filled with peanut butter or frozen meat, though if I am really anxious, I may not eat it until you return. Put some music on the radio, and if you are going out in the evening, leave a light on. You can also give me one of your old jumpers that smells of you.

Don't make a fuss of me before you depart, just be calm and quiet, and do the same when you return. I know this is hard because my welcome is so effusive. After all I love you wildly – who else is so thrilled to see you when you have only been out for five minutes? However, if my behaviour is causing issues, this will help me to understand that calm is good, and that your going out and returning is no big deal.

We dogs read our owner's movements, so we know when you grab your coat, your bag and your keys you are going out. If we react badly to this, you can work with us by going through the process of leaving, but then return just a few moments later. If you keep doing this, we will not get as anxious because we won't be sure you are actually leaving. You want to promote a calm atmosphere. Ignore me when you leave, and for a few minutes when you return.

If the problem is severe, please take me to a trainer, or behaviour specialist, who can really help us to achieve a peaceful and happy life together.

Aggression

We labradors are an easy-going bunch. We like, or can learn to like, most people, dogs and other creatures.

However, things can go a bit awry if I am not properly socialized, or if I have a dominant personality, or indeed if I am being flooded with testosterone. As mentioned earlier, young male dogs have to get used to other dogs responding to them very differently as they grow into adulthood, and you may have a few hiccups. If you suspect hormones are the problem and you don't like the idea of neutering me unnecessarily (thank you for that consideration), vets can chemically castrate a dog, a treatment which is effective for around a year, before you decide whether or not surgery is the solution.

If I bark and lunge at other dogs, you need to divert my attention back to you. When you see another dog coming, get a treat in your hand and distract me with the treat so that I focus on you, instead of obsessing about the advancing pooch. If I have been attacked or bitten by another dog, this may also make me more inclined to be suspicious of other dogs, and you will have to work on my socialization by building up my trust in other dogs

and encouraging calm behaviour. Remember, if I see another dog with its hackles up, I am more likely to respond in kind. Always work to promote calm behaviour.

Ultimately, you are responsible if I bite or attack another dog, and you can be fined for not keeping me under proper control. If you are struggling, please seek professional help at the earliest opportunity – your vet is a good place to start. If a placid and friendly labrador suddenly becomes aggressive, take them to the vet to get checked out – it may be indicative of an undiagnosed physical problem.

The real secret to dog training is to understand that it is not something you ever, ever, ever stop doing. You can train me to sit and lie down on command, to wait and to stay exactly as instructed, but the one thing you can guarantee, if you don't keep up the training, is that I won't carry on behaving beautifully. Having said that, I am a lovable, loyal labrador and you will be amazed at what I can learn to do.

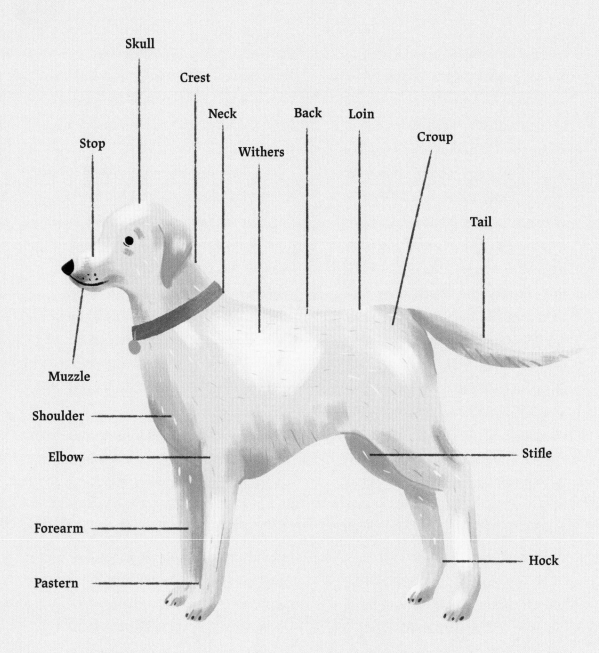

Skull

Crest

Neck

Back

Loin

Croup

Withers

Stop

Tail

Muzzle

Shoulder

Elbow

Stifle

Forearm

Hock

Pastern

Diet

I love you. I really, really do love you more than anything else in the world, except possibly FOOD. It's hard to explain just quite how much I adore eating. I mean the smell – I can almost taste it. I will eat anything, quite literally ANYTHING; even poo can hold considerable temptation for me. I know you don't like me doing this, but frankly I simply don't understand why not, I mean the taste is … well it is hard to describe, but I like it! More of this later … (see page 61).

Mealtimes are my favourite time of the day. I treat each meal as a race, even if I am an only dog. I will gobble up my food in seconds, barely tasting it. This is not good for me. Special food bowls are available from pet shops that make it harder for me to eat quickly. I have to work to access the food in these bowls, using my tongue to tease out every last bit, and this slows down the rate at which I eat.

Basically, when it comes to food, I have no stop button. If you accidentally leave the top off a box of kibble, I will attempt to eat every last morsel. I will eat until I can barely drag my bloated carcass to the sofa. On the plus side, my phenomenal appetite means that I respond beautifully to food-based

training techniques, especially if it means pleasing you at the same time – that is a double bonus for me.

If you are using a lot of treats in training, remember to deduct the overall amount from my meal allowance. This way my treats are just part of my daily rations. I am so eager to please you that once I have grasped the basics, you can try rewarding my good behaviour with methods that won't add inches to my waistline.

Labradors are adept at emotional blackmail. When you are dining, we will plant ourselves beside you, slavering, gazing up at you with big, round, pleading eyes. We are willing you to slip us a morsel of something. If you do, we will love you even more. However, much as I hate to admit it, this is not a sensible approach. Our propensity to overeat and gain weight means that the simplest and safest approach is never, ever, to feed us from your plate. Be firm from the start; the simplest technique is to send me into another room while you are eating.

Being the food provider puts you in a position of great power, so use that power responsibly. Of course, you can ignore my advice and feed me scraps from your plate, but if you do this, you need to give me less food at my mealtimes to counteract these extra calories. Are you really prepared to try to work out the precise nutritional impact of those three scraps of chicken and half a roast potato, four crisps and a piece of cheese scone, and deduct the equivalent calories from my dinner? I thought not.

I don't blame you for wanting to feed me from the table, but unless you are extremely disciplined with my overall food intake it is *incredibly* bad for me. I will gain weight and this will shorten my life. In addition, labradors are prone to a range of weight-related health issues; indulge me and you could be condemning me to years of ill health and pain. The old adage 'a moment on the lips, a lifetime on the hips', could have been written for a labrador.

Please don't feed me straight after a walk. Let me rest for half an hour before feeding. This is important: I can develop a twisted stomach or bloat which is very dangerous. Always leave an interval after exercise before feeding me and this problem shouldn't occur.

Weight

Labradors are big, well-muscled, powerful dogs with a thick coat. We are not a bony breed and as already stated, with our huge appetites it is easy for us to gain weight. If I am only fed at mealtimes and I get a minimum of two hours exercise a day, you should not have a problem with my weight.

Male labradors should weigh somewhere from 27 to 36kg (60–80lb) and females from 25 to 34kg (55–75lb). However, this is not a hard-and-fast rule; some dogs have a bigger build, and some are small for the breed. American labs tend to weigh a little less than their English cousins. Muscle weighs more than fat, so a super-fit, heavily muscled working dog may weigh more than one that is carrying too much fat, but one is a healthy dog and the other is not. Our stature may be solid, but we should still have a waist and although you shouldn't be able to see our ribs, you should be able to feel them if you run your hands along our sides.

As with you humans, carrying extra weight can lead to other health problems, including diabetes and hip dysplasia. A high-fibre, low-fat complete food diet, with fewer calories per pound, can be utilized to help me shed some pounds; I won't feel cheated if you feed me this. Alternatively, you can just cut back on portions of my regular food. If you can help get me back into shape I will enjoy exercise more, and that will in turn help maintain my proper figure.

All dogs are omnivores, eating both plant and animal matter to survive. However, it's not good for us to eat anything and everything.

DO NOT give your labrador any of these foods:

- **Alcohol** isn't much good for humans and it's not good for labradors either. As well as all the obvious symptoms of alcohol poisoning – sickness and diarrhoea – it can also damage my central nervous system.

- **Avocado** contains persin, a fungicidal toxin that is harmless to humans, but which can cause vomiting and diarrhoea in dogs. It is present in the seed, the fruit, the skin and the leaves.

- **Caffeine** is not good for dogs. If we consume excessive amounts, it can have a similar effect to chocolate. Don't give us coffee or tea.

- **Chocolate** contains a compound called theobromine; it is fine for humans who can process it, but it can kill all dogs, even in small amounts. If your labrador

has eaten chocolate, call the vet straight away and ask for advice. Note how much chocolate has been consumed and whether it is dark or milk chocolate; dark chocolate contains more theobromine. Depending on how much chocolate has been consumed, the vet may want to make your labrador vomit, and they may administer charcoal to absorb the poison.

- **Cooked bones** are highly dangerous. They can splinter and damage your labrador's internal organs, often causing perforation of the gut. Raw bones are safe, but only give your labrador a large raw bone, as small raw bones can cause choking.

- **Corn-on-the-cob** is not poisonous to dogs, but it can cause a blockage in our intestines and be potentially fatal.

- **Grapes, sultanas and raisins** can cause liver damage and kidney failure in some dogs. It is impossible to predict whether or not your labrador might be affected, so do not give us grapes, sultanas or raisins, and please think twice before you offer me a morsel of carrot cake or fruit cake!

- **Macadamia nuts** are toxic to dogs and can cause severe pain, muscle tremors and limb paralysis.

- **Onions, garlic and chives,** indeed anything from the onion family, are toxic to dogs and can cause serious gastrointestinal irritation and red blood cell damage.

- **Xylitol** is an artificial sweetener used in many low-fat and diet products, which is highly toxic to all dogs, including labradors. It can induce hypoglycaemia, or low blood sugar, and is linked to liver failure and blood-clotting disorders.

Nutrition

There is a huge variety of commercial dog food on the market and there is an increasingly sophisticated selection of products on offer: wheat intolerance, gluten intolerance, hypoallergenic, vegan and sensitive tummies, all are catered for. You can feed your labrador a purely dry diet, a mix of wet and dry, cook your own meals, have freshly cooked frozen meals delivered to your door, or follow the unfortunately named BARF (Biologically Appropriate Raw Food) diet.

If you study the labels, you will find it hard to make direct comparisons of the nutrient content between the different forms of dog food. Protein and fat are important components, as is a balance of vitamins and minerals. Labradors need different quantities of nutrients at different stages of their lives; puppies have a much higher protein diet and the requirements of senior dogs (seven years and above) are different to that of a lively adult labrador.

High-quality foods generally contain less in the way of fillers and more nutritional ingredients; cheaper foods will use more fillers to satisfy appetite.

Most adult dog foods contain around 20–30 per cent protein (5–8 per cent in wet foods) and 9–14 per cent fat (2–4 per cent in wet foods). Dietary fibre (vegetable matter) maintains intestinal health, helps to treat both constipation and diarrhoea and has a probiotic function. Ash is a measure of the mineral content of food and includes calcium, copper, iron, magnesium, manganese, phosphorus, potassium, selenium and zinc. There are 13 vitamins that are important for health: vitamin A, vitamin C, vitamin D, vitamin E, vitamin K and eight B vitamins.

Protein usually comes in the form of meat and fish, but vegetables can also supply proteins, and these protein sources are cheaper. Protein from non-meat sources, such as soya, maize and potato, are harder for a dog to digest and in some instances can cause dietary intolerance. Raw-meat BARF diets have a much higher protein content and, as the meat is uncooked, it retains its nutrients. The nature of the protein content in dog food can vary from pure meat to rendered meat meal, bone or animal derivatives.

Fats and oils are important for a labrador's skin and fur and are also a good source of energy. Some essential fatty acids, such as omega-3, which are also important for health, are often added to commercial dog food.

Fillers make up the remaining percentage of dog food. This is likely to include wholegrains, such as wheat, barley, corn, rice, oats, rye and sorghum, many of which also include important nutrients. They may also include peas, potatoes, sweet potatoes, quinoa and lentils, which are higher in calories.

As with all food purchases, you get what you pay for, but your labrador may well be perfectly happy with a competitively priced dog food. If you are concerned about quality, don't rely on the front of the packaging for information; look at the ingredients. However, If your labrador starts to get tummy upsets or skin conditions you may have to pay more attention to her diet.

Always be guided by your vet. Dogs are less likely to develop food allergies than humans – they have robust digestive systems – allergies to surroundings are more common

irritants. However, anecdotal evidence suggests that labradors may be more prone to food allergies than some other breeds of dogs. Seek professional advice if I develop a skin disorder or have regular tummy upsets – don't assume it's a food allergy.

Complete food, a specially formulated diet in the form of kibble, is perhaps the simplest way to ensure that your labrador gets a nutritionally balanced diet. If it is kept in an air-tight container it has a good shelf life.

Wet food, in the form of tins or pouches, is usually served with biscuits or kibble to ensure all the nutritional requirements are met.

The BARF diet imitates the diet a dog would have in the wild and is high in protein. It consists of 60–75 per cent raw meat and bones, which can be in the form of items such as chicken wings and necks, or raw fish. The remaining 25–40 per cent consists of fruit and vegetables, offal, eggs or dairy food and is made up by you to create the nutritional whole. To make life simpler, manufacturers now sell the meat part of this diet, which is delivered frozen; portions can then be defrosted as required. You have to be quite committed to put me on this diet: it's not cheap and requires a lot of proactive food preparation. If you choose to feed me the BARF diet, please follow all the usual hygiene precautions.

In many countries around the world, you can also buy specially prepared, nutritionally appropriate, cooked meals online, which are then delivered frozen to your door. This is a premium product. I will love it, but it doesn't come cheap.

Wind

One of the reasons labradors may be prone to wind is that we gobble our food up so quickly. If I am frequently contaminating your air space with noxious fumes, first try feeding me twice a day and buy a bowl designed to make me eat more slowly. If you think a food intolerance could be the problem, consult your vet.

Water

Please make sure I always have water available and wash my water bowl daily. Please keep some water in the car for me and a travelling water bowl so that you can always offer me a drink. I often badly need some refreshing water at the end of a walk.

Gourmet Poo

Coprophagia, or eating poo, is not a problem for me – you are the one that has a problem with it. All puppies may well try eating poo out of pure curiosity. Bitches lick their puppies' bottoms to encourage urination and defecation, and when the business is done, they eat everything up to keep the nest clean. This is natural instinct. Some dogs only eat poo in their own back garden, which could also be seen as a form of nest cleaning. Other dogs have a particular fondness for rabbit poo, sheep poo or horse poo.

Eating poo is not bad for us *per se*, as long as we are regularly wormed. The main issue is that it tests the relationship between dog and owner; humans find it repulsive. Punishing me won't work – I simply don't understand what the problem is, and I never will. Dietary additives (such as pineapple) are very rarely effective either.

First and foremost, pick up all poo in the garden as soon as it is deposited – if it's not there, I can't eat it.

As with all behavioural issues, the best approach is a reward-based training scheme. You will need to keep my top favourite treats to hand for this – chicken, cheese or sausages will usually suffice; this needs to be a seriously tasty treat to distract me. You can prepare a word that you will use only in this situation. Attract my attention, use the word, throw down the food and keep your fingers crossed. It might not work initially, but keep at it. Little by little, I should lose interest and race towards my special treat. This system requires real perseverance on your part. Alternatively, work on reinforcing my 'Leave' training.

Some people muzzle their poo-eating labs on walks, but we can still get our muzzles into the poo and lick it with our tongues anyway.

If you give me a dental chew stick in the garden after a walk that should clean my mouth quite effectively; neither of us want you to shrink away from me when I come up for a pat or want to give you a doggy kiss!

First Aid and Health

I feel faintly embarrassed that so much emphasis seems to be placed on my tendency to run too fat – can I help it if I love my food? However, obesity is one of the biggest threats to the health of a labrador. Slipping us illicit treats from your plate may feel like an expression of love, but actually it is a bit like offering an alcoholic a drink: one leads to another. Don't show your love by giving me excess treats – it is not a kindness.

If you stick to this rule, use treats for training purposes only and give me plenty of exercise, you should have a happy, healthy labrador. My thick coat protects me from getting cut as easily as other breeds as I trot around exploring and I have a robust, well-muscled physique. My eyes should be bright, my nose damp, and my coat thick and glossy.

I believe I have already mentioned that we are quite possibly the most popular dog breed in the world, constantly topping the rankings. The downside to this has been the development of the breed from a fairly small gene pool. There are a number of genetic conditions that labradors are prone to, though breeders are now attempting to eliminate them by

the careful genetic testing of dogs and bitches for these conditions before they are put to stud. If you have followed advice and purchased me from a reputable breeder, my chance of getting these problems is considerably reduced. You can find more information on these and other disorders later on in this chapter. However, you might want to consider taking out health insurance for me, as some of these problems are very expensive to treat.

First-Aid Kit

Your canine first-aid kit should include:

- Antiseptic wipes
- Pressurized saline wound wash
- Antiseptic cream suitable for dogs
- Sterile gauze dressings
- Self-adhesive bandages
- A dog boot, in case of cut or injured paws.

Pills and Medicine

Please don't ever give me any form of human medicine unless my vet specifically suggests it and advises the dosage.

Prescribed liquid medication is fairly easy to administer if you have a little doggy medicine syringe – nine times out of ten this comes with the medicine. The dose will be specified and marked on the syringe. Fill up the syringe to the required mark, then pop it into the side of my mouth, pointing the syringe toward my throat, and squeeze quickly. This is usually a straightforward operation.

Pills can be more of a challenge. You can try holding my body gently between your legs, get the pill in one hand and with the other lift my head upwards and open my mouth. You want to drop the pill towards the back of my throat. Hold my jaws closed and stroke my throat to encourage me to swallow.

This may be easier with me than other dog breeds because of my enthusiasm to eat anything and everything. Some pills come in dog-friendly flavours and if you act like you are giving me a great treat I may be convinced, but if I am not fooled try one of the following techniques. If I generally have dry food, you can try popping the pill into some wet food and giving me that to eat.

Alternatively, utilize something slightly moist, such as cream cheese or pâté to, quite literally, sweeten the pill. Pop the pill inside a little ball of something delicious, again act like you are giving me a treat, get me to sit and offer the camouflaged pill – the chances are we will wolf it down. Processed human foods are not good for us, but small amounts can be used in extremis.

Cuts

Be warned, the first time I injure myself it may look worse than it is, but try not to panic. If I have been running my heart will be beating fast, and I will be pumping blood out of my cut with some velocity. The first thing to do is to get me to sit down to slow my heartbeat. This will allow you to assess the severity of the injury. Apply gentle pressure to the cut.

If you are unsure, please contact the vet straight away for advice, lift me in and out of the car and don't let me do anything active until I have been checked out. If stitches are required, the sooner this is done the better, although I won't thank you. The vet will have to anaesthetize me and may need to keep me in overnight. I will be very wobbly after an anaesthetic, and you may well have to help me into the house. Help me onto my bed or onto the sofa so I can be close to you. I will sleep.

I will also need the 'cone of shame' (buster collar), or a medical pet shirt, because I will not leave stitches or dressings alone. I must not be allowed to worry at my stitches, though I don't understand why you won't allow me to. These specially designed devices prevent me from doing any damage to myself, despite my best attempts. If I am stuck with a buster collar, I will try to get it off, but persist. Leave it on at night to be on the safe side or you will wake to find I have removed my dressing and all of my stitches, which will require another trip to the vet, which is costly for you and traumatic for me. Be firm.

The collar can come off on walks and for meals – I will be able to access my

water bowl with it on no matter what I would have you believe. Medical vests just come off for walks and toilet breaks.

If my foot has been injured, you may have to cover it with some kind of plastic shoe so that the dressing doesn't get wet – even in summer the grass is covered with dew in the morning.

I will be on lead walks for a minimum of ten days; the vet will guide you. They will want to give me regular check-ups to ensure that everything is healing as it should, and any dressings will need to be changed regularly. Even if I seem to be healing nicely, don't let me off the lead until the vet gives me the all-clear. I can rip stitches open if I am allowed to run free.

Heat Exhaustion

All dog owners should be aware that you must not leave us in cars in full sun or even in the shade when it is hot. Although it may not feel that warm, a car can heat up very quickly. Conservatories and caravans can also be dangerous. When it is 22°C (72°F) outside, the interior temperature of a car can quickly rise to 47°C (117°F).

To keep us safe, it is best not to leave us in the car alone at all. Even with the best intentions, even five minutes can be too long, because as you humans know, shops can have queues, or you can bump into someone you know, and before you know it half an hour has passed and I am dying due to the heat.

You should be careful when you travel with me on long journeys. Give me frequent breaks, the chance to stretch my legs, relieve myself, have a drink and relax in the shade.

We can also get heat exhaustion on a summer walk if you allow us to run too much. Ball fanatics won't stop chasing after a ball you are throwing for us because we are getting too hot. If there is no water nearby, we will have no way of cooling down. If I seem disorientated, confused or start to sway, I have become dangerously overheated.

The first thing to do is to cool me down. Spraying me with a hose will be too much of a shock to my system. Instead, wet a large towel with cold water and place it over me. Gently sprinkle cold water over the towel every few minutes to keep it cool – a watering

can with a sprinkler head on will do the job perfectly. Overheating to this extent can cause long-term damage and I should be checked out by the vet. It can take me a few days to recover from heat exhaustion.

This is a shocking experience for me and for you, so please don't let me run around like a mad thing on a hot day. Exercise me first thing in the morning, or late in the evening when it is cooler.

Diarrhoea

If I have diarrhoea, the chances are that either you have made a dramatic alteration to my diet, which may not suit me, or, and this is the more likely of the two, that I have scavenged something to eat that has not agreed with me. As stated on page 53, we labradors are greedy and like nothing more than chomping on something illicit we find on a walk.

The first course of action is to withhold food for a day, but please make sure I have water on hand, as diarrhoea can lead to dehydration. After 24 hours feed me something bland: cooked chicken with boiled rice is ideal.

I will enjoy this! Just give me a small portion and allow me plenty of time to digest it before giving me a little bit more. This will usually sort everything out and I can return to normal feeding. However, if things don't improve, please take me to the vet.

If you see blood in my faeces, or if I am vomiting as well, contact the vet straight away.

Vomiting

I will vomit sometimes – all dogs do you know. Sometimes this may be because I have gobbled my food down too quickly. If this happens you will probably be horrified to see me happily tucking in to eat the whole regurgitated mess all over again. Greedy puppies are especially prone to this, so if it happens regularly, feed me the same amount but split it into smaller portions more times a day. Don't let me tear around straight after eating.

I quite like to eat grass, but I may vomit after eating it; this is nothing to worry about.

If I vomit repeatedly, I may have eaten something unpleasant. Follow the same

Boston

Owned by Aimee | Lives in Cheshire | @boston_the_brave

Boston is a 3-year-old Fox Red Labrador. He
is the most loving, loyal and family-orientated
dog. His ball and food/treats are life! He is very
mischievous but life would be boring without him.

principle of withholding food for 24 hours, and then feeding me a bland diet, as for diarrhoea, above. If things don't improve, take me to the vet.

If you notice something resembling blood, or faecal matter in my vomit– and that smells really foul – take me straight to the vet.

Coughing

A very occasional cough is nothing to worry about, but a regular cough should be checked out by my vet.

Kennel cough is an airborne disease, usually a virus, that easily spreads between dogs. I can be inoculated annually against kennel cough and the vaccination will lower my chances of catching it and reduce my symptoms if I do. Most boarding kennels insist that I am inoculated against kennel cough before a stay. If I am not vaccinated, I can pick up kennel cough from infected dogs. Most dogs with kennel cough aren't too poorly, but some of us can be badly affected and may need anti-inflammatories to bring down our temperature and reduce inflammation.

You will need to keep me away from other dogs for 2–3 weeks after my symptoms have disappeared. Don't let me race around if I have kennel cough, as this can make symptoms worse. Instead, give me gentle exercise on a lead.

A cough can also be indicative of heart disease, especially if it happens after exercise or in the evening. Get me checked out by a vet who will listen to my heart to see if there's an issue.

Ears

My ears hang down like long pendants, keeping the interior warm, so are perfectly designed to incubate all kinds of fungal and bacterial infections. To help prevent these problems, you can lift up my ears and dry the inside with a cotton ball after I have been swimming.

If I start scratching my ear or shaking my head, have a look inside: there may be grass seed, a burr or some other foreign body that is causing discomfort. If you can see something obvious, remove it gently – damp cotton wool is good for this. Don't probe further into the ear or use ear buds. If the foreign body doesn't lift out easily, I will need a trip to the vet.

If you can see a dark discharge in the ear that looks like coffee grounds, I may have ear mites. If my ear is red, I may have an infection, and once again a trip to the vet is in order. Over-the-counter products are not recommended: please consult an expert.

Skin Irritation

Skin allergies can have a number of trigger factors: oversensitivity can be caused by fleas (see more in Chapter 6), pollen, grass, moulds, house dust mites and some foods. The skin becomes itchy, red and can be hot to the touch. Bald patches and skin infections can develop. Please make an appointment for me to see the vet if you are concerned; skin problems tend to get worse if they are left untreated and the vet will help you to determine what my trigger factors might be.

Lick granuloma is a self-inflicted condition caused when we lick one spot repeatedly until the fur is removed and the area around it becomes raised and sore. Sometimes this is caused by psychological issues, such as separation anxiety, but don't assume this is the

case. I might have a bacterial infection or some kind of allergy. Guess what? A trip to the vet is in order!

Bites

If you own a dog, any dog, the chances are that at some point they will become involved in some nose-to-nose power posturing. We labradors generally don't look for trouble, but we can be quite vocal, full of sound and fury, signifying nothing. This, combined with our size, can make other dogs nervous. The good news is that our thick coats can provide a fair amount of protection, but if we do get bitten, you should get us checked out, as we may need a shot of antibiotics to make sure the wound doesn't get infected.

Wasps and Bees

Labradors, just like humans, will suffer irritation if we are stung by wasps or bees. First, check to make sure that the sting itself is not still stuck in my skin. If it is, remove it carefully, scraping it out rather than pulling, as this can release more venom. Bathe the area with cool water to help reduce the swelling. Most

dogs suffer minor pain and irritation, however, if the area is swelling rapidly or if your dog is having difficulty breathing or vomiting, take it straight to the emergency vet.

Snake Bites

Snake bites can be fatal. In the UK it is only the adder that can cause labradors serious harm, but in countries such as America and Australia, there are more venomous snakes that can strike. If you see your labrador worrying something in the grass, call it to you immediately.

The majority of snake bites occur during the spring and summer months. If you think your labrador has been bitten, keep him quiet and calm and take him to the vet as a matter of urgency. If you see the snake attack, make a note of its markings as this will help the vet administer the correct antivenom. You can tie a constricting band above the bite to slow the spread of the venom. This should be snug but not too tight.

Fireworks

You humans seem to expect us labradors to be immune to noise, given

Snake-bite Symptoms

If you are worried your dog may have been bitten by a poisonous snake, symptoms to look out for include:

- A small wound with fang marks
- Swelling of the affected area
- Collapse (though they can recover temporarily)
- Sudden weakness
- Vomiting
- Hypersalivation
- Dilated pupils
- Twitching of the muscles.

that we work as gun dogs. However, let me disabuse you of that notion. Working dogs are trained to ignore noises, but without that training we will respond as any other dog to fireworks - with blind terror. Prevention is the best cure: don't ever take me to a firework display and don't let me be outside if you hear fireworks being let off nearby.

If I wasn't frightened by fireworks before, I will become hypersensitive to them if I am near some that are going off.

If you know there are going to be fireworks in the vicinity of your home, keep me indoors. Take me for a good walk before it gets dark, so that I won't need toilet breaks during the evening. Turn up the volume on the television or the radio to drown out the noise, and don't leave me alone. Stay calm and ignore any bangs to reassure me.

You can try desensitizing therapies to gradually get me accustomed to strange noises. Suitable sounds can be downloaded online, and you can play them to me, carefully controlling the volume, starting quietly. This is a slow process, I should not be alarmed at any stage, but become gently acclimatized to the sounds. Play with me and feed me with this quiet noise in the background. Little by little, over the course of a few weeks, you can raise the volume and I will learn that this is not a threatening sound.

If my phobia is severe, the vet can recommend some natural therapies and possibly pheromone treatments to make me feel more secure. Tranquilizers are a very last resort, but even these won't cure the terror, just make us very sleepy.

Genetic Issues

Labradors can be at risk of certain inherited genetic conditions, so it is good to be aware of them.

Hip dysplasia

This is caused when the hip ball and socket is poorly developed, and the joint becomes unstable. Signs of dysplasia usually become apparent between five and 18 months of age.

Instances of hip dysplasia are falling. However, even with parental checks, genetics can play a part and dysplasia can still be a problem for labradors. Treatment is mostly directed toward preventing further deterioration, reducing inflammation and easing pain. Weight loss can help if obesity is an issue, and rest and controlled exercise are beneficial. Hydrotherapy and physiotherapy may be recommended. Surgery can be an option in some cases.

Hip Displasia Symptoms

If you are worried your dog may have hip displasia, symptoms to look out for include:

- Limping and lameness
- Difficulty getting up
- Difficulty walking uphill
- Waddling gait
- Reluctance to exercise or climb stairs.

Elbow Displasia Symptoms

If you are worried your dog may have elbow displasia, symptoms to look out for include:

- Reluctance to exercise
- Front paws pointing outwards, or elbows held at a peculiar angle
- Swollen elbows.

Elbow dysplasia

Like hip dysplasia, elbow displasia is caused by abnormal development, but in this instance it affects the elbows. Signs of dysplasia usually show between five and 18 months of age. It causes pain, swelling and instability; arthritis develops in time.

Treatment includes rest and controlled exercise; hydrotherapy and physiotherapy can be beneficial, together with weight control, pain relief and sometimes surgery.

Progressive Retinal Atrophy (PRA)

Tests can determine whether or not dogs carry this mutated gene; labradors are not the only breed affected by this condition. It can lead to degeneration in vision and, at worst, to blindness. There is no cure for this disease; DNA testing is the best hope for gradual eradication. If your dog seems to be unsure in the dark or starts bumping into things, take her to the vet to be checked.

Grooming

Ihave a very thick, double-layered waterproof coat. It's why I love swimming, whatever the weather. The undercoat is short and fluffy and acts as an insulating layer, a bit like a wet suit. The outer layer consists of longer, sleeker, waterproof hairs that help shield the undercoat. Add to all this the fact that my coat is naturally oily to help repel water, not to mention my webbed toes and otter-like tail that serves as a rudder, and you can understand why I am always keen for a dip.

In theory, my coat is relatively low maintenance, and a brush once or twice a week will suffice for most of the year. However, twice a year I will shed my undercoat. Do not underestimate how dramatic this shed will be – you can expect great balls of hair, like tumbleweed, blowing around the house. At this time, you will need to groom me daily to help remove the shedding hairs before they deposit themselves all over you, your furniture and your house.

This twice-yearly shed allows me to lose my heavy winter coat in spring to acquire my sleeker summer coat. Then, as temperatures fall, I lose my summer coat and grow a warm, thick winter coat. It is particularly important

to groom me daily when I am shedding as the discarded hairs can tangle in my coat and trap dead skin cells and excess oils. This will make me uncomfortable and can cause itchy skin and dermatitis.

Working labradors that live in outside kennels tend to have a well-defined shed, but domestic pets sometimes extend their period of shed, which may well be due to the fact that most of us live in centrally heated environments.

Don't imagine that this heavy, twice-yearly shed means that labradors don't shed hair the rest of the year too. That is definitely not the case; we shed hair all year round, it's just it's even more dramatic twice a year. If you want to share your life with a lab, you had better be comfortable with dog hair being something of a feature of your home décor.

Before you ask, all labradors shed in the same way, whatever the colour of our coat.

Bathing

I love bathing and will happily fling myself into water at any given opportunity. However, I am not discerning when it comes to the location; muddy or stagnant water is as inviting to me as a clear mountain stream. In consequence, labradors do tend to carry the aroma of wet dog, which is quite pungent in our case. Please dry our ears after we have been for a swim or been given a bath; our ears hang down, maintaining a warm moist environment inside the ear, and as a result we can develop ear infections.

As with all breeds of dog, it is not good for labradors to be bathed too often, and in theory we don't need much bathing. What can be a bit of an issue, however, is our fondness for applying a dab of other interesting scents around our necks and behind our ears. We do like to roll in pongy things, particularly fox poo or, indeed, any other form of animal excrement.

If I have been rolling in mud, you might get away with just hosing me down. Some breeds of dog are averse to this technique, but I usually tolerate it with equanimity. However, in some instances more stringent measures are called for.

If you need to bathe me, wet me thoroughly and then apply a dog

shampoo – a human shampoo can give me skin irritation – and give me a good rub all over to clean my fur. Rinse me gently, making sure you remove all traces of the shampoo, as any residue will cause irritation. Please avoid getting any water in my ears – it might trigger an ear infection. If possible, don't wet my face at all. It can be cleaned separately with a clean cloth dipped in warm water and then wrung out.

Once I am clean, have lots of warm towels to hand. Put one on the floor, put me onto it then put another towel on top of me. Rub me briskly – I will enjoy this. When you release me, I will run wildly all over the house in a state of high excitement and rub myself on your carpets and soft furnishings to dry myself off further. If it's not cold, let me into the garden and I will race around until I feel like myself again.

Grooming us will help us to keep ourselves clean, and if you use the right equipment, we will enjoy the experience. Regular brushing stimulates blood circulation and spreads the natural oils through my coat, which should help ensure I look wonderfully

glossy. This is also a good opportunity for you to give me a once-over and make sure I am healthy with no unexplained lumps and bumps.

I have such a thick coat that you may need a selection of grooming tools to keep it in tip-top condition. A bristle brush is always handy and is a gentle way to introduce puppies to being groomed. It is also effective for removing dust and dirt from my coat. A rubber curry brush is good for when I am having a bath, because it gently dislodges dirt and loose hair. Many lab owners also use a medium to large slicker brush, which has multiple rows of small, flexible pins and is designed to help remove my loose undercoat when I am shedding, though this should only be used in places where my hair is longer, such as around my rump. Be gentle when you use this – please don't scrape it against my skin.

Check-up

When you have groomed me, please give me a check-over to make sure my eyes are bright. Clean away any debris in the corners of my eyes with some

damp cotton wool. Remember that our floppy ears don't allow air to circulate readily and can fall prey to infections. For more detailed instructions on ear care, see pages 70-71.

Smile Please!

You can help to keep my teeth clean by giving me raw bones to chew, or you can buy specially designed chews that are supposed to help prevent the build-up of plaque and tartar. Feeding me with dry food and hard dog biscuits is also helpful.

If I develop bad breath, this may indicate gum disease and a serious build-up of tartar will require the vet to give my teeth a deep clean. This has to be done under anaesthetic. It's an unnecessary expense for you and I certainly won't enjoy the experience. What's more, neglecting my teeth can lead to the development of other serious health problems.

You can also clean my teeth every couple of days. I know this sounds crazy! Use a special dog-friendly toothpaste, which tastes of meat, so I don't mind the experience. Do not use human toothpaste on me – it can be harmful. To start with, gently rub the toothpaste over a couple of my teeth to get me used to the sensation. Gradually increase the amount of toothpaste and the time spent on the task over a week or so. If you get me used to you manipulating my lips you will be able to reach all areas of my teeth. Either use a small toothbrush or a specially designed finger-brush that slips over your finger to clean my teeth. Give me plenty of treats to reward me for cooperating.

Ask the vet to check my teeth occasionally, perhaps when I go in for my annual inoculation, just to make sure no problems are developing.

Pedicure

My nails grow like yours and shouldn't be allowed to get too long. Pavement walking helps to keep them in shape, but you will still need to trim them. Get someone who knows how to show you how to perform this task before trying it at home. If you are not confident, leave nail-trimming to the professionals.

My nails contain the quick which includes the vessel that brings blood to the nails. If you cut my nails too short you will cut this; it will be painful and I will bleed. It will also mean I won't want you to come anywhere near my nails again.

If you can hear my nails clicking when I walk across a hard floor, this is a sign that they are too long. Long, uncut nails can lead to lameness.

A little and often is the best policy for pedicures. If you trim my nails every two weeks, you will only need to take off a small piece of the nail. I will be suspicious of this process initially but in time I will relax and behave while you give me my pedicure. You will become more confident in performing this procedure and will be able to cut a little closer to the quick.

When you are giving me a pedicure and have a hold of my paw, take the opportunity to examine my pads and my webbed toes to make sure everything is in good shape.

Labradors are not vain dogs. We don't mind a bit of mud, but nevertheless we will let you tidy us up; as a general rule, whatever makes you happy makes us happy!

Tiny
Companions

All animals accommodate a host of tiny friends and with my fabulously thick, double-layered coat, there are plenty of places for all kinds of things to hide!

Fleas

As sure as night follows day, I will get fleas. Fleas are everywhere; cats and humans shouldn't get too squeamish about them, because you have your own cat fleas and human fleas too. I can pick them up from another dog, a cat, your home, your friend's home or from your clothes or your shoes.

These tiny parasites are superb jumpers, which is how they hop from their environment, to host, to home, to host and so on. Females must have a meal of blood before they lay their eggs and can lay up to 50 eggs per day. The eggs are like tiny grains of sand, they fall off me when they are laid and then hatch into larvae within 2–5 days. The larvae, which are around 0.5cm (¼in) long, live in carpets, soft furnishings and cracks in the floorboards. They feed, and after around two weeks build a cocoon, from which they emerge as adult fleas when a food source is nearby. The life cycle takes around 3–4 weeks. Fleas can also pass on tapeworms to me.

Fleas are particularly active when the weather is warmer, but they can still reproduce inside the home in winter. Moreover, fleas can lie dormant in a home for a long time when there is no food source, but the arrival of a pet stimulates them to hatch. If you are moving house, make sure my flea treatments are up to date.

Dog fleas prefer dogs, cat fleas prefer cats, but they will hop on any host in extremis, even you! If you are being bitten by fleas it suggests that our home has a serious flea problem.

If I have fleas, bear in mind that only approximately 5 per cent of the flea population will be on me; the remaining 95 per cent will be in our home! Spot-on treatments, which are very effective, only kill the adult fleas, so if there is an infestation it can take up to three months to eradicate the problem. The best solution is to consistently use appropriate preventative flea treatments from the moment I come into your life as a puppy.

Puppies require specific flea treatments suitable for their age and weight; the earliest this can be administered is usually at eight weeks. Some treatments are not suitable for young puppies, so you should always consult your vet for advice. Fleas can trouble puppies badly; they can have an adverse reaction to flea bites leading to allergic dermatitis, and in severe infestations a puppy can develop life-threatening anaemia.

How can you tell whether I have fleas? Scratching is a tell-tale sign, but you can see evidence of fleas too: part my coat at the back of my neck, or near my ears, or at the base of my tail and look for tiny black specks that resemble pepper. This is flea dirt, basically digested blood. If you put this on a piece of paper and dampen it, it will turn red and this is proof that I have fleas.

Chemical spot-on treatments, which are administered to the back of the neck and between the shoulder blades, are very effective. These will also kill all the flea eggs. Live fleas will be killed within 24 hours and some flea treatments also kill ticks.

Please remember to wash my pet bedding regularly, hoover floors thoroughly and don't forget the soft furnishings. Empty the contents of the dust bag after hoovering!

If you follow this regime, fleas should never become a problem. However, if you do let things slide and your house has a serious flea infestation – you will probably be being bitten too at this point – you will also need to use a chemical spray treatment on your house to help kill the pesky things.

If you want to use 'natural' herbal preparations, please check with your vet first. Ironically, the ingredients in some products are not safe for use around dogs or cats. Cat flea treatments are not safe for use on dogs either and vice versa!

Ticks

Like fleas, ticks will climb onto me when I am out on a walk, then enjoy a drink of my blood. The tick will stay in place until it has had enough to drink when it will drop off. Quite apart from being unsightly, ticks can cause severe skin irritation and can also transmit Lyme disease or borreliosis, which is a tick-transmitted bacterial infection that occurs in Europe, North America and

Lyme Disease Symptoms

These might include:

- Fever
- Lethargy
- Limping
- Swollen lymph nodes (situated in the neck, chest, the tops of the front legs, groin and behind the knees of the rear legs).

Asia, and which can affect humans as well as dogs.

Ticks are very common in areas where there is wildlife or livestock and are most commonly seen in warmer weather. They start off very small but grow as they feed. You are unlikely to spot them in my thick coat, but you can feel them as small flat lumps. Part my fur and take a closer look.

Ticks resemble a skin tag and can be light in colour, grey or quite dark. The part you can see is the tick's large, flat body (if you look very closely you can see its legs). Don't attempt to pull it

Amber

Owned by Jess and family | Lives in Essex | @amber_jemxoxo

Amber is a happy and loyal companion who
never fails to put a smile on our faces. She loves
fetching a ball just as much as she loves kisses
and cuddles!

straight off me – this can result in cross contamination as parts of the mouth can remain *in situ*.

Ticks are easily removed with a tick tool, which allows you to anchor the body of the tick, while you then twist the tool. This effectively unscrews the tick from its food source. Once you have removed the tick, squash it very hard between some paper and dispose of the body. It is best to purchase a tick tool when you get a puppy, so you always have it to hand when needed. You can buy a cheap tick tool from most pet shops. Vaccinations against Lyme disease are now available if you are concerned that I am at high risk.

If you are worried that I may have contracted Lyme disease from a tick, take me to the vet.

Worms

Dogs can and will pick up worms from numerous sources: soil, vegetation or faeces can be contaminated with worm eggs, and contaminated fleas can pass on tapeworms to your dog. Worms can be transmitted from dog to dog via their faeces and though it is unusual, it can also be passed on to you. This is another good reason for all dog owners to pick up that poo!

Worms can cause diarrhoea and vomiting, weight loss, weakness, coughing and anaemia. Puppies with worms develop an abnormally swollen tummy. If you see me scooting – dragging my bottom along the floor – this is an indication that I may have worms, though I can do this for other reasons too, so get me checked out by the vet.

Intestinal Worms

- **Roundworms** are passed on to a puppy via its mother's milk and adult dogs can contract them from contaminated soil or meat. These look like spaghetti in your dog's poo, but spaghetti that wriggles around!

- **Hookworms and whipworms** live in my intestines, where they latch on with sharp teeth to suck my blood. Weight loss is a common symptom and I contract them via contaminated soil.

- **Tapeworms** are spread by infected fleas. They can also be spotted around my anus and look like grains of rice in my poo but are actually small segments of the tapeworm. I pick them up if I accidentally ingest an infected flea while grooming myself. As the flea is digested, the tapeworm egg is released and hatches, whereupon it latches onto my small intestine. Occasionally an entire tapeworm can be passed or vomited up – not a pleasant experience for anyone, so keep on top of my flea control!

its larvae, which are found in infected slugs, snails and frogs. Dogs can accidentally eat small slugs if they are on their toys or their fur. The lungworm moves through the dog's body and finally settles in the heart and blood vessels. We excrete the larvae in our poo. This infects more slugs and snails, which in turn can infect more dogs. Take your dog to the vet to be checked out if they are displaying any of the symptoms below; the vet will need to prescribe a special course of medication to eliminate lungworm. In some areas where lungworm is especially prevalent it is advisable to give your dog preventative medication.

All dogs should be regularly wormed, and there are numerous deworming medications available. Puppies are at particular risk from worms but please seek advice from your vet before worming your puppy.

Lungworm

Lungworm (*Angiostrongylus vasorum*), is fairly common in some countries and it can kill. I can contract it if I consume

Lungworm Symptoms
These might include:
- Coughing
- Breathing problems
- Reluctance to exercise
- Abnormal blood clotting

Heartworm

Dirofilariasis is an infection caused by parasites of the genus *Dirofilaria* and is transmitted via the bite of an infected mosquito. It affects dogs, cats and ferrets. It is found in large swathes of the USA and Canada but is rarely seen in the UK. There are 30 species of mosquito that transmit it. Heartworm kills dogs, but as it takes several years before symptoms appear, the disease is often well-advanced by the time clinical signs are visible. Blood tests can confirm a diagnosis and X-rays will show the extent of the damage. Medication is given via a series of injections. It is critical that dogs are kept quiet during treatment and for several months afterwards. If you live in an area where heartworm can be contracted, preventive medication is recommended.

Heartworm Symptoms

These might include:

- Dry cough
- Shortness of breath
- Listlessness
- Loss of stamina

Mites and Mange

These two conditions are uncomfortable rather than life-threatening but can be costly for you and distressing for us, so as with many things, prevention and regular treatment are the rules here.

Mites

- **Ear mites** (*Otodectes cynotis*), are common in cats but can affect dogs too, so if your dog has ear mites always check their feline friends as well. The parasites live in the outer ear canal. Symptoms included ear scratching and shaking of the head so that the ears flap. The ear will become red and inflamed and you may see a waxy brown discharge. Untreated ear mites can lead to other ear infections. The ear will need to be regularly cleaned and treated with medicated ear drops prescribed by the vet. Regular flea treatment should act as a preventative.

- **Fur mites** (*Cheyletiella spp.*) cause cheyletiellosis, commonly dubbed 'walking dandruff'. These small, white mites live on the surface of the skin and cause mild itchiness; one of the obvious signs of a fur-mite infestation is a coat full of small flakes of skin or scurf.

- **Harvest mites** (*Trombicula spp.*), are small orange mites that can also affect cats and humans. They can easily be picked up in grassy areas or woodland in late summer and autumn. This mite causes intense itching and inflammation in the feet and lower legs, but it can also affect the armpits, the tummy, the genitals and very occasionally the ears; scratching the itch can lead to infections. It can be seen with the naked eye and it is easily treated with an insecticide; anti-inflammatories may be required to ease discomfort. Regular flea treatments should deal with this problem without it ever becoming an issue.

Mange

There are two types of skin mites that can cause mange: *Demodex canis* and *Sarcoptes scabiei*.

A dog with a good immune system should not fall prey to demodectic mange, but puppies can be at risk as they cannot stop the parasite and it is usually passed from mother to pup. The parasite lives within the hair follicles and causes the skin to become very itchy, which can lead to hair loss and lesions can develop. It spreads from the point of infection and across the whole body; the dog's skin appears to turn a blue-grey. You won't be able to see these parasites with the naked eye – they can only be seen through a microscope. This form of mange does not easily spread to other dogs or to humans, and is treated with a topical preparation.

Scabies, however, is highly contagious. I don't have to come into direct contact with another creature to catch it. All dogs in the household will need to be treated with a medicated shampoo. This is a zoonotic disease, which means it can be passed on to humans. Foxes are a common source of contagion.

Fascinating Labrador Facts

- **The first Andrex labrador** puppy advertisement appeared in 1972, and puppies have featured in 130 different ads since then.

- **The first registered** yellow labrador, Ben of Hyde, was born in 1889.

- **Two labrador** guide dogs, Salty and Roselle, helped lead their owners to safety in the attack on the Twin Towers in New York on 11 September 2001.

- **The UK Guide Dogs** for the Blind Association is supported entirely by public donations. From birth to retirement, it costs around £55,000 to support a single guide dog.

- **Paul McCartney's** black labrador, Jet, is thought to have inspired the Wings' song 'Jet'.

- **During the Covid-19** lockdown of 2020, sports commentator Andrew

Cotter's videos of his two labradors, Olive and Mabel, went viral, attracting over 40 million views.

- **The labrador breed's** origins are in the Canadian province of Newfoundland. St John's water dogs, famed for their prowess in the water, came to Britain with sailors from trading ships working between Canada and Poole in Dorset. These dogs were bred with British hunting dogs, most notably by the Earl of Malmesbury, and the Dukes of Buccleuch and Home. The labrador retriever was thus developed in Britain in the 1830s.

- **The Duke of Buccleuch's** black labrador Buccleuch Avon is considered the foundation dog of the modern breed.

- **The labrador** has been the most popular dog breed in the USA since 1991.

- **Labradors have webbed** toes and are enthusiastic swimmers.

- **Five labrador retrievers** have received the People's Dispensary for Sick Animals (PDSA) Dickin Medal, the highest award an animal can receive for serving in military conflict.

- **Labradors, like perfumers**, have superb noses and rank among the top ten dogs with the best sense of smell. They can sniff out drugs and explosives, undertake search and rescue, and are now being trained to detect health issues, warning of low blood sugar levels, tumours and oncoming seizures.

Index

Further Reading

Cotter, Andrew, *Olive, Mabel & Me*, Black & White Publishing, 2020

Fogle, Ben, *Labrador*, William Collins, 2015

Garfield, Simon, *Dog's Best Friend*, W&N, 2021

Kaiser, Claudia, *Labrador Training*, Expertengruppe Verlag, 2019

Mattinson, Pippa, *The Labrador Handbook*, Ebury Press, 2015

Moore, Asia, *The Happy Labrador*, Worldwide Information Publishing, 2019

Pearce, Paul Allen, *Think Like A Labrador*, Paul Allen Pearce, 2014

Roy, Malini, *The Dog Lover's Pocket Bible*, PB Pocket Bibles, 2009

Whitwam, Linda, *The Complete Labrador Handbook*, ISBN- 13: 978- 1542648233, 2017

Acknowledgements

Thanks must go to Jimmy the Lurcher, our first family dog, who turned this cat-loving, dog-hating mother-of-two into an ardent dog-worshipper. We grew up together and he seduced me, batting his long blonde eyelashes and generally behaving abominably. Jimmy was a living, breathing incarnation of a badly behaved dog and together we discovered how dog training can transform your life.

Every dog owner will get to know numerous Labradors as they walk their dogs. I must thank my chum Sarah Gristwood for giving me the chance to get to know her two labs, Bruno and Louis. She trusted me with dog-sitting duties and I was introduced to the charms of lab ownership. I must also thank James Fuller who patiently explained the finer points of training Labradors. His three working labs are phenomenally well behaved.

I must thank my husband, Eric, without whose patient nagging I would never have discovered that dog-owning was a good thing. Our children, Florence and Teddy, have patiently endured their parents' dog-worshipping tendencies and embraced the delights of dog walking in the rain. They are the first to point out if the house ever smells of dog.

Florence must also be thanked for taking the time to proofread the first draft of this book. Despite being very busy and important, she patiently corrects my punctuation and makes all kind of helpful suggestions.

At Batsford I must, as always, thank Polly Powell for her faith in me. Lilly Phelan has been the kindest and gentlest of editors and a delight to work with and Gemma Doyle must be thanked for her superb design.